OCTOPUS

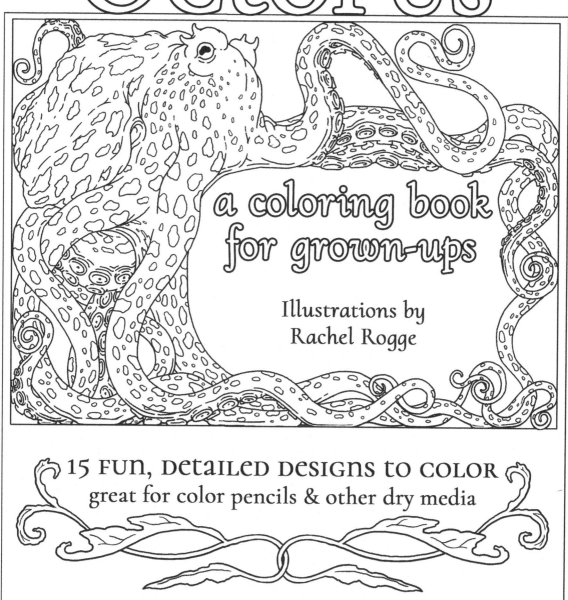

a coloring book
for grown-ups

Illustrations by
Rachel Rogge

15 FUN, DETAILED DESIGNS TO COLOR
great for color pencils & other dry media

Octopus: a Coloring Book for Grown-ups

ISBN-13: 978-1539083061

GREETINGS!
Thanks for choosing this book!
If you are fascinated by octopus, this coloring book is for you! In it, you will discover fifteen fanciful drawings celebrating these intelligent invertebrates.

INSTRUCTIONS
Carefully remove one of the included blank pages from the back of this book with scissors or a sharp paper knife to use between pages while coloring, or use an extra sheet of paper of your own to protect the other pages from embossing or bleed-through.

This book is best suited for use with dry media such as color pencils.

Relax, have fun, and embrace your creativity!
Enjoy!

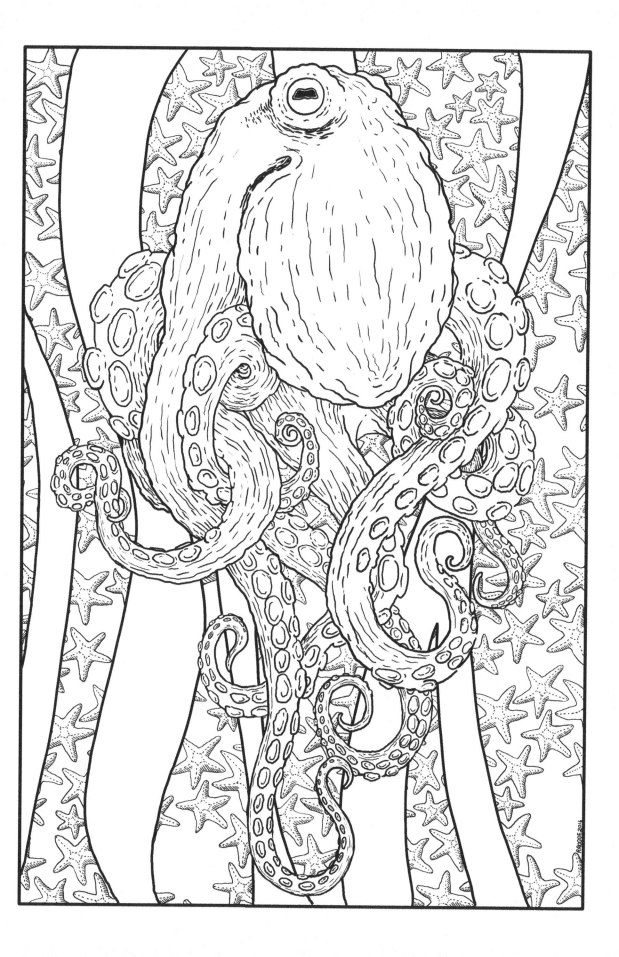

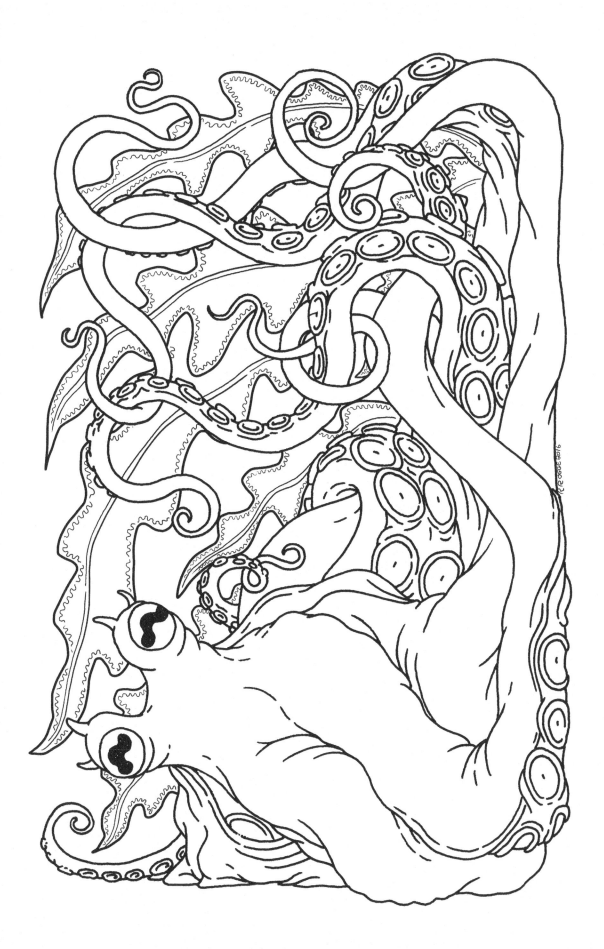

R ROGGE 2016

ABOUT THE ILLUSTRATOR

Rachel Rogge (pronounced "rogue-he") studied art history, science illustration and biology in California. She has worked as a science illustrator since 2003, mainly focusing on art production and development in educational publishing. She has illustrated two children's books in the Nature's Yucky! series. Rachel lives in the Pacific Northwest with 2 humans, a dog, a cat, and a leopard gecko. She is a big fan of cephalopods and loves drawing them. This is her first coloring book, but probably not her last.

Her website can be found at www.pensandbeetles.com.

Made in United States
Orlando, FL
25 November 2022

24993327R00024